The Leader's Book of Inspiration

MICHAEL J. ELLIOTT

The Leader's Book of Inspiration

Quotes and Insights for Today's Leaders

Dedicated to God, Father of Mercies to Whom all things are owed.

CONTENTS

INTRODUCTION

BY MICHAEL J. ELLIOTT

Leaders—our nations, religions, wars and mythologies have been defined by them; and even in the 21st century, this has not changed.

"The history of the world is but the biography of great men."
— *Thomas Carlyle*

Throughout history, awe-inspiring leaders have impacted our lives in more ways than we could ever imagine. They have woven themselves into the fabric of our consciousness. We tell their stories, we read their biographies, and we debate their place in history. Our myths and legends usually include leader archetypes that are often presented as "heroes."

The greatest of leaders can make the seemingly impossible, possible. Alexander the Great united the Greek city-states and led them across the Aegean Sea to defeat the largest empire the world had yet seen.
Remarkable leaders lay a foundation where there is none. They see what is not readily apparent to most. They bring out the best in their followers, inspiring positive change. The Founding Fathers of America sought to create a better form of government--one without kings or popes. The republic they

founded would become the global ideal, and would set America apart as the greatest nation in the world.

Exceptional leaders inspire entire chapters in the lives of their people. They can raise nations out of ruins. The very best leaders make an everlasting impression on humanity's collective soul. Is it any wonder we continue to return to their words and carrying them with us perpetually in our hearts and minds?

How to Use This Book:

Let this book serve as an inspiration and reminder of your great potential. Whenever you find yourself in doubt of your ability to accomplish your goals, use this book as a guide back to self-actualization.

Remember, you are not defined by your failures, nor are you defined by your successes. You are defined by your beliefs, as your life will closely reflect them. It is my hope that this book will help you create new beliefs that will lead to more accomplishments.

Where There is Wisdom There is Harmony

This book is an embodiment of the saying "a wise man learns from every person he meets." Enclosed is borrowed wisdom from different types of leaders in various fields, for it is not enough that we learn only from business and political leaders — we must go beyond the modern image of a leader and learn from greats in spheres that are not typically associated with leadership.

I. Cornerstone

Christ and the Apostles, teach us the most important of all lessons: although the path ahead may be dark, we must continue on, firmly holding on to faith. When all odds are stacked against us, we have to steadily press on. This is the foundational lesson all great leaders must learn.

II. Light in the Darkness

From **the poets,** we learn that each of us has a creative side, and no matter how chaotic life may get, we must nurture that part of ourselves. It is through our creativity that we will find the ability to inspire both ourselves, and others, in unconventional ways.

III. The Crown and Scepter

The monarchs of old, remind us of the value   of decisive leadership and the disastrous consequences of unchecked power.

IV. Pen, Paper & Destiny

Authors show us again and again that the pen is mightier than the sword. We are compelled to reflect on the monumental importance of the written word and its ability to carry knowledge and experience from one generation to the next.

V. Folk Wisdom

Proverbs, remind us of the ancient wisdom that flows in our veins and sleeps in our bones.

VI. Charting the Course

National leaders reveal, to raise a nation to new heights, one must be the embodiment of the highest ideals.

VII. When Art Speaks

Artists and composers remind us of the great debt we owe to those who create lasting works of profound impact. They help us see that we can accomplish anything.

VIII. Philosopher's Stone

Philosophers encourage us to develop, exercise and constantly maintain our love of learning--to continually stoke the flames of intellectual curiosity, while always continuing our quest for personal development.

IX. May Your Intentions Be Noble

Visionaries teach us to always work towards the ideal. And to do so effectively, we must awaken our ability to dream.

Make it your business to learn

Seek out all of the names in this book (especially the ones you don't know). Examine their successes, failures, and their life's work to glean everything possible to further your growth as a leader.

Many things that are now deemed "possible," began as "impossible." May this book be your continual reminder that your dreams—no matter how big—are indeed attainable.

Introduction

I
Cornerstone:
Book of Divinity

God ultimately raises up leaders for one primary reason: His glory. He shows His power in our weakness. He demonstrates His wisdom in our folly. We are all like a turtle on a fence post. If you walk by a fence post and see a turtle on top of it, then you know someone came by and put it there. In the same way, God gives leadership according to His good pleasure.

-Matt Chandler

What we plant in the soil of contemplation, we shall reap in the harvest of action.
-Meister Eckhart

Give your mind to prayer with humility and with great peace.
-Saint Ailbe

Better to illuminate than merely to shine, to deliver to others contemplated truths than merely to contemplate.
-Thomas Aquinas

Patience is the companion of wisdom.
-Saint Augustine

For those who exalt themselves will be humbled, and those who humble themselves will be exalted.
-Jesus Christ

We must alter our lives in order to alter our hearts, for it is impossible to live one way and pray another.
-William Law

Joan of Arc

One life is all we have and we live it as we believe in living it. But to sacrifice what you are and to live without belief, that is a fate more terrible than dying.
-Joan of Arc

Start by doing what's necessary; then do what's possible; and suddenly you are doing the impossible.
-Francis of Assisi

Peace if possible, truth at all costs.
-Martin Luther

The greatest wisdom in a man is to refrain from injurying another when he has the power to do so.
- Saint Teilo

Teresa of Avila

The tree that is beside the running water is fresher
and gives more fruit.
-Teresa of Avila

Beware of no man more than of yourself; we carry our
worst enemies within us.
-Charles Spurgeon

Conscience is the chamber of justice.
-Origen

If you are kind, people may accuse you of ulterior
motives. Be kind anyway.
-Mother Teresa

It is not your outward appearance that you should beautify, but your soul, adorning it with good works.
-Clement of Alexandria

The greater and more persistent your confidence in God, the more abundantly you will receive all that you ask.
-Albertus Magnus

You are not only responsible for what you say, but also for what you do not say.
-Martin Luther

Right is right even if no one is doing it; wrong is wrong even if everyone is doing it.
-Saint Augustine

The higher the hill, the stronger the wind: so the loftier the life, the stronger the enemy's temptations.
-John Wycliffe

The price of inaction is far greater than the cost of making a mistake.
-Meister Eckhart

He that hath no rule over his own spirit is like a city that is broken down, and without walls.
-Proverbs 25:28

In this life we cannot always do great things. But we can do small things with great love.
-Mother Teresa

If we strive for goals, relishing in the pleasure of circumstance, nothing is enjoyable, and life becomes purposeless.
-Andrew the Apostle

Do not become a disciple of one who praises himself, in case you learn pride instead of humility.
-Mark the Evangelist

I am not afraid... I was born to do this.
-Joan of Arc

Do not be afraid, for we have God as our guide and helper. God will guide as God pleases.
-Saint Brendan

Be intent upon the perfection of the present day.
-William Law

The things that we love tell us what we are.
-Thomas Aquinas

Where there is charity and wisdom, there is neither fear nor ignorance.
-Francis of Assisi

Even if I knew that tomorrow the world would go to pieces, I would still plant my apple tree.
- Martin Luther

Where there is no vision, the people perish.
-Proverbs 29:18

Think not that humility is weakness; it shall supply the marrow of strength to thy bones. Stoop and conquer; bow thyself and become invincible.
-Charles Spurgeon

It is only through shadows that one comes to know the light.
-*Saint Catherine of Siena*

Love the truth. Let others have their truth, and the truth will prevail.
-*Jan Hus*

A tree is known by its fruit; a man by his deeds. A good deed is never lost; he who sows courtesy reaps friendship, and he who plants kindness gathers love.
-*Saint Basil*

Jesus Christ

Thou shalt love the Lord thy God with all thy heart,
and with all thy soul, and with with all thy mind.
This is the first and great commandment. And the
second is like unto it, Thou shalt love thy neighbor as
thyself. On these two commandments hang all the
law and the prophets.
-*Jesus Christ*

II
Light in the Darkness:
Book of Poets

The great poet is a great artist. He is painter and sculptor.
The greatest pictures and statues have been painted and
chiseled with words. They outlast all others.

-Robert G. Ingersoll

We have committed the Golden Rule to memory; let us now commit it to life.
-Edwin Markham

It is better to have dreamed a thousand dreams that never were than never to have dreamed at all.
-Alexander Pushkin

Be still my heart; thou hast known worse than this.
-Homer

Edwin Markham

This is the miracle that happens every time to those
who really love: the more they give, the more they
possess.
-Rainer Maria Rilke

My strength is as the strength of ten, because my
heart is pure.
-Alfred Lord Tennyson

Keep your face always toward the sunshine - and
shadows will fall behind you.
-Walt Whitman

Trust in dreams, for in them is hidden the gate to
eternity.
-Khalil Gibran

You may not control all the events that happen to
you, but you can decide not to be reduced by them.
-Maya Angelou

It takes courage to grow up and become who you
really are.
-e. e. cummings

They who dream by day are cognizant of many things which escape those who dream only by night.
-*Edgar Allan Poe*

Genius... is the capacity to see ten things where the ordinary man sees one.
-*Ezra Pound*

Do not wait to strike till the iron is hot; but make it hot by striking.
-*William Butler Yeats*

Gratitude bestows reverence, allowing us to encounter everyday epiphanies, those transcendent moments of awe that change forever how we experience life and the world.
-John Milton

Anxiety is the handmaiden of creativity.
-T. S. Eliot

The same ambition can destroy or save, and make a patriot as it makes a knave.
-Alexander Pope

The most pitiful among men is he who turns his
dreams into silver and gold.
-*Khalil Gibran*

Failure is in a sense the highway to success, as each
discovery of what is false leads us to seek earnestly
after what is true.
-*John Keats*

Do not seek to follow in the footsteps of the wise.
Seek what they sought.
-*Matsuo Basho*

If you don't like something, change it. If you can't
change it, change your attitude.
-*Maya Angelou*

Lives of great men all remind us we can make our
lives sublime, And departing, leave behind us
Footprints on the sands of time.
-*Henry Wadsworth Longfellow*

What man does not understand, he fears; and what
he fears, he tends to destroy.
-*William Butler Yeats*

"Come to the edge," he said.
"We can't, we're afraid!" they responded.
"Come to the edge," he said.
"We can't, We will fall!" they responded.
"Come to the edge," he said.
And so they came.
And he pushed them.
And they flew."
— *Guillaume Apollinaire*

Freedom lies in being bold.
-Robert Frost

Self-reverence, self-knowledge, self-control; these
three alone lead one to sovereign power.
-Alfred Lord Tennyson

Where the way is hardest, there go thou; Follow your
own path and let people talk.
-Dante Alighieri

Once in Persia reigned a king
Who upon his signet ring
Graved a maxim true and wise,
Which if held before the eyes
Gave him counsel at a glance
Fit for every change and chance.
Solemn words, and these are they:
"Even this shall pass away."
-Theodore Tilton

The proper study of Mankind is man.
-Alexander Pope

A ruler should be slow to punish and swift to reward.
-Ovid

The future enters into us, in order to transform itself in us, long before it happens.
-Rainer Maria Rilke

We convince by our presence.
-Walt Whitman

If you aren't in over your head, how do you know
how tall you are?
-*T. S. Eliot*

Perplexity is the beginning of knowledge.
-*Khalil Gibran*

The true genius shudders at incompleteness - and
usually prefers silence to saying something which is
not everything it should be.
-*Edgar Allan Poe*

III
The Crown & Scepter:
Book of Kings

There can be no failure to a man who has not lost his courage, his character, his self-respect, or his self-confidence. He is still a king.

-Orison Swett Marden

A leader is a dealer in hope.
-Napoleon Bonaparte

The things you think about determine the quality of your mind. Your soul takes on the color of your thoughts.
-Marcus Aurelius

There is nothing impossible to him who will try.
-Alexander the Great

Napoleon Bonaparte

What is the good of experience if you do not reflect?
-Frederick the Great

Fear not, we are of the nature of the lion, and cannot descend to the destruction of mice and such small beasts.
-Elizabeth I

In the day of prosperity be joyful, but in the day of adversity consider.
-King Solomon

There is little that can withstand a man who can conquer himself.
-*Louis XIV*

It takes less courage to criticize the decisions of others than to stand by your own.
-*Attila the Hun*

I beg you take courage; the brave soul can mend even disaster.
–*Catherine the Great*

I came, I saw, I conquered.
-*Julius Caesar*

I am not afraid of an army of lions led by a sheep; I am afraid of an army of sheep led by a lion.
-*Alexander the Great*

He who defends everything defends nothing.
-*Frederick the Great*

Pharaoh Akhenaton

True wisdom is less presuming than folly. The wise
man doubteth often, and changeth his mind; the fool
is obstinate, and doubteth not; he knoweth all things
but his own ignorance.
-Akhenaton

It is not death that a man should fear, but he should fear never beginning to live.
-*Marcus Aurelius*

It is impossible to please all the world.
-*Louis XIV*

My own soul is my most faithful friend. My own heart, my truest confidant
-*Babur*

When I give a minister an order, I leave it to him to
find the means to carry it out.
-Napoleon Bonaparte

As iron sharpens iron, so a friend sharpens a friend.
-King Solomon

Nothing is impossible to a valiant heart.
-Henry IV of France

For in prosperity a man is often puffed up with pride, whereas tribulations chasten and humble him through suffering and sorrow. In the midst of prosperity the mind is elated, and in prosperity a man forgets himself; in hardship he is forced to reflect on himself, even though he be unwilling. In prosperity a man often destroys the good he has done; amidst difficulties he often repairs what he long since did in the way of wickedness.

-Alfred the Great

Alfred the Great

No society can prosper if it aims at making things easier-instead it should aim at making people stronger.
-*Ashoka*

A clear and innocent conscience fears nothing.
-*Elizabeth I*

We write our names in the sand: and then the waves roll in and wash them away.
-*Augustus Caesar*

IV
Pens, Paper & Destiny:
Book of Authors

A creation of importance can only be produced when its author isolates himself, it is a child of solitude.

-Johann Wolfgang von Goethe

Deprived of meaningful work, men and women lose their reason for existence; they go stark, raving mad.
-Fyodor Dostoevsky

Do not go where the path may lead, go instead where there is no path and leave a trail.
-Ralph Waldo Emerson

We are what we believe we are.
-C. S. Lewis

Fyodor Dostoevsky

Great things are done when men and mountains
meet.
-William Blake

You cannot create experience. You must undergo it.
-Albert Camus

You can't wait for inspiration. You have to go after it
with a club.
-Jack London

Follow your bliss and the universe will open doors
where there were only walls.
-*Joseph Campbell*

We cannot live only for ourselves. A thousand fibers
connect us with our fellow men.
-*Herman Melville*

Faithless is he that says farewell when the road
darkens.
-*J. R. R. Tolkien*

It is the nature of man to rise to greatness if greatness
is expected of him
-John Steinbeck

Virtue is bold, and goodness never fearful.
-William Shakespeare

Dream no small dreams for they have no power to
move the hearts of men.
-Johann Wolfgang von Goethe

When you acknowledge the integrity of your
solitude, and settle into its mystery, your
relationships with others take on a new warmth,
adventure and wonder.
-*John O'Donohue*

Hope is the things with feathers that perches in the soul, and sings the tune without words, and never stops at all.
-Emily Dickinson

Circumstances do not make the man, they reveal him.
-James Allen

The two most powerful warriors are patience and time.
-Leo Tolstoy

All that is gold does not glitter, not all those who wander are lost; the old that is strong does not wither, deep roots are not reached by the frost.
-*J. R. R. Tolkien*

There is wisdom of the head, and wisdom of the heart.
-*Charles Dickens*

The Plays of William Shakespeare by Sir John Gilbert

Love all, trust a few, do wrong to none.
-William Shakespeare

A man without ethics is a wild beast loosed upon
this world.
-Albert Camus

The more tranquil a man becomes, the greater is his
success, his influence, his power for good. Calmness
of mind is one of the beautiful jewels of wisdom.
-James Allen

We must let go of the life we have planned, so as to
accept the one that is waiting for us.
-Joseph Campbell

If you fell down yesterday, stand up today. *-H. G. Wells*

If you want to conquer fear, don't sit home and think about it. Go out and get busy.
-Dale Carnegie

The mind has exactly the same power as the hands; not merely to grasp the world, but to change it.
-Colin Wilson

Faith is a grand cathedral, with divinely pictured windows - standing without, you can see no glory, nor can imagine any, but standing within every ray of light reveals a harmony of unspeakable splendors.
-Nathaniel Hawthorne

They who have conquered doubt and fear have conquered failure.
-James Allen

When people talk, listen completely. Most people never listen.
-Ernest Hemingway

Always prefer the plain direct word to the long, vague one. Don't implement promises, but keep them.
-C.S. Lewis

Let me never fall into the vulgar mistake of dreaming that I am persecuted whenever I am contradicted.
-Ralph Waldo Emerson

The grand essentials to happiness in this life are something to do, something to love, and something to hope for.
-Joseph Addison

To live without hope is to cease to live.
-Fyodor Dostoevsky

Live your beliefs and you can turn the world around.
-Henry David Thoreau

The further a society drifts from truth the more it will
hate those who speak it.
-George Orwell

Love not what you are but only what you may
become.
-Miguel de Cervantes

Man is made by his belief. As he believes, so he is.
-Johann Wolfgang von Goethe

The more violent the storm, the quicker it passes.
-Paulo Coelho

It is better to fail in originality than to succeed in imitation.
-Herman Melville

It's the job that's never started as takes longest to finish.
-J. R. R. Tolkien

What lies behind you and what lies in front of you,
pales in comparison to what lies inside of you.
-Ralph Waldo Emerson

The sole meaning of life is to serve humanity.
-Leo Tolstoy

Great minds have purposes; others have wishes.
-Washington Irving

Courage is not simply one of the virtues, but the form of every virtue at the testing point.
-C. S. Lewis

But man is not made for defeat. A man can be
destroyed but not defeated.
-Ernest Hemingway

As a man is, so he sees. As the eye is formed, such
are its powers.
-William Blake

The greatest achievement was at first and for a time
a dream. The oak sleeps in the acorn, the bird waits
in the egg, and in the highest vision of the soul a
waking angel stirs. Dreams are the seedlings of
realities.
-James Allen

V
Folk Wisdom:
Book of Proverbs

The wisdom of the wise and the experience of the ages is preserved into perpetuity by a nation's proverbs, fables, folk sayings and quotations.

-William Feather

It is absurd that a man should rule others, who cannot rule himself.
-*Latin Proverb*

Not the cry, but the flight of a wild duck, leads the flock to fly and follow.
-*Chinese Proverb*

Rough waters are truer tests of leadership. In calm water every ship has a good captain.
-*Swedish Proverb*

Who begins too much accomplishes little.
-German Proverb

Habits are first cobwebs, then cables.
- Spanish Proverb

The best time to plant a tree was 20 years ago. The next best time is now.
-Chinese Proverb

We learn to walk by stumbling
- Bulgarian Proverb

Without perseverance talent is a barren bed.
-Welsh Proverb

A wise man remembers his friends at all times; a
fool, only when he has need of them.
-Turkish Proverb

If you want to be respected, you must respect
yourself.
-Spanish Proverb

Worry often gives a small thing a big shadow
- *Swedish Proverb*

Words have no wings but they can fly a thousand miles.
-*Korean Proverb*

Better one day as a lion than a hundred as a sheep.
-*Italian Proverb*

Water does not run under a lying stone.
-*Russian Proverb*

Faults are thick where love is thin.
-Danish Proverb

Do not protect yourself by a fence, but rather by your
friends.
-Czech Proverb

A book holds a house of gold.
-Chinese Proverb

A rolling stone gathers no moss.
-French Proverb

The master of the people is their servant.
-Yemeni Proverb

The best candle is understanding.
-Welsh Proverb

They that sow the wind, shall reap the whirlwind.
-Scottish Proverb

Praise loudly, blame softly.
-Russian Proverb

A gentle hand may lead even an elephant by a hair.
-Iranian Proverb

Vision without action is a daydream. Action without vision is a nightmare.
-Japanese Proverb

A ruler must sometimes humor as well as command.
-Unknown

A slip of the foot may soon be recovered; but that of the tongue perhaps never.
-Danish Proverb

VI
Charting the Course: Book of Patriots

We know what we are, but know not what we may be.

-William Shakespeare

It is absolutely necessary...for me to have persons
that can think for me, as well as execute orders.
-George Washington

You have enemies? Good. That means you've stood
up for something, sometime in your life.
-Winston Churchill

We must support our rights or lose our character,
and with it, perhaps, our liberties.
-James Monroe

George Washington

Leadership and learning are indispensable to each other.
-John F. Kennedy

A chip on the shoulder is too heavy a piece of baggage to carry through life.
-John Hancock

The only limit to our realization of tomorrow will be our doubts of today.
-Franklin D. Roosevelt

John F. Kennedy

Keep your eyes on the stars, and your feet on the ground.
–Theodore Roosevelt

If your actions inspire others to dream more, learn more, do more and become more, you are a leader.
–John Quincy Adams

In periods where there is no leadership, society stands still. Progress occurs when courageous, skillful leaders seize the opportunity to change things for the better.
–Harry Truman

In matters of style, swim with the current; in matters of principle, stand like a rock.
-*Thomas Jefferson*

Leadership consists of nothing but taking responsibility for everything that goes wrong and giving your subordinates credit for everything that goes well.
-*Dwight D. Eisenhower*

You cannot escape the responsibility of tomorrow by evading it today.
-*Abraham Lincoln*

Liberty will not long survive the total extinction of morals.
-*Samuel Adams*

An ignorant people is the blind instrument of its own destruction.
-*Simon Bolivar*

But you must remember, my fellow-citizens, that eternal vigilance by the people is the price of liberty, and that you must pay the price if you wish to secure the blessing.
-*Andrew Jackson*

Disciplining yourself to do what you know is right
and important, although difficult, is the highroad to
pride, self-esteem, and personal satisfaction.
-Margaret Thatcher

Always stand on principle....even if you stand alone.
-John Adams

A well-instructed people alone can be permanently a
free people.
-James Madison

Nearly all men can stand adversity, but if you want to test a man's character, give him power.
-*Abraham Lincoln*

All men are by nature born equally free and independent.
-*George Mason*

Honesty is the first chapter in the book of wisdom.
-*Thomas Jefferson*

Abraham Lincoln

The credit belongs to those who are actually in the arena, who strive valiantly; who know the great enthusiasms, the great devotions, and spend themselves in a worthy cause; who at best know the triumph of high achievement; and who, at worst, if they fail, fail while daring greatly, so that their place shall never be with those cold and timid souls who know neither victory nor defeat.
-*Theodore Roosevelt*

I know not what others may choose but, as for me, give me liberty or give me death.
-*Patrick Henry*

You are not here merely to make a living. You are here in order to enable the world to live more amply, with greater vision, with a finer spirit of hope and achievement. You are here to enrich the world, and you impoverish yourself if you forget the errand.
-*Woodrow Wilson*

Discipline is the soul of an army. It makes small numbers formidable; procures success to the weak, and esteem to all.
-*George Washington*

The spirit of envy can destroy; it can never build.
-*Margaret Thatcher*

Nothing in this world can take the place of persistence. Talent will not: nothing is more common than unsuccessful men with talent. Genius will not; unrewarded genius is almost a proverb. Education will not: the world is full of educated derelicts. Persistence and determination alone are omnipotent.
-Calvin Coolidge

Take time to deliberate; but when the time for action arrives, stop thinking and go in.
-Andrew Jackson

The price of greatness is responsibility.
-Winston Churchill

Winston Churchill

All the great things are simple, and many can be expressed in a single word: freedom, justice, honor, duty, mercy, hope.
-Winston Churchill

Nothing can stop the man with the right mental attitude from achieving his goal; nothing on earth can help the man with the wrong mental attitude.
-Thomas Jefferson

Do what you can, with what you have, where you are.
-Theodore Roosevelt

Character is like a tree and reputation like a shadow. The shadow is what we think of it; the tree is the real thing.
-*Abraham Lincoln*

Subtlety may deceive you; integrity never will.
-*Oliver Cromwell*

There is a price tag on human liberty. That price is the willingness to assume the responsibilities of being free men. Payment of this price is a personal matter with each of us.
-*James Monroe*

VII
When Art Speaks:
Book of Zeal

No great artist ever sees things as they really are. If he did, he would cease to be an artist.

-Oscar Wilde

Country Road in Provence by Night by Vincent van Gogh

Great things are done by a series of small things
brought together.
-Vincent Van Gogh

Learn all there is to learn, and then choose your own
path.
-George Frideric Handel

Trifles make perfection, and perfection is no trifle.
-Michelangelo

It's on the strength of observation and reflection that one finds a way. So we must dig and delve unceasingly.
-*Claude Monet*

Just as iron rusts from disuse, even so does inaction spoil the intellect.
-*Leonardo Da Vinci*

Inspiration is a guest that does not willingly visit the lazy.
-*Pyotr Ilyich Tchaikovsky*

The greatest danger for most of us is not that our aim
is too high and we miss it, but that it is too low and
we reach it.
-Michelangelo

The meaning of life is to find your gift. The purpose
of life is to give it away.
-Pablo Picasso

One should never forget that by actually perfecting
one piece one gains and learns more than by starting
or half-finishing a dozen.
-Johannes Brahms

Portrait of an Old Man in Red by Rembrandt

Practice what you know, and it will help to make
clear what now you do not know.
-Rembrandt

Wolfgang Amadeus Mozart

In spite of everything, I shall rise again
-*Vincent Van Gogh*

Ceaseless work, analysis, reflection, writing much,
endless self-correction, that is my secret.
-*Johann Sebastian Bach*

All I insist on, and nothing else, is that you should
show the whole world that you are not afraid. Be
silent, if you choose; but when it is necessary,
speak—and speak in such a way that people will
remember it.
-*Wolfgang Amadeus Mozart*

Even in poverty I lived like a king for I tell you that
nobility is the thing that makes a king
-Ludwig van Beethoven

Young people can learn from my example that
something can come from nothing. What I have
become is the result of my hard efforts.
-Joseph Haydn

VIII
Philosopher's Stone:
Book of Wisdom

What is it that is most beautiful? – The universe; for it is the work of God. What is more powerful? – Necessity; because it triumphs over all things. What is most difficult? – To know one's self. What is most easy? – To give advice. What method must we take to lead a good life? – To do nothing we would condemn in others. What is necessary to happiness? – A sound body and a contented mind.

-Thales

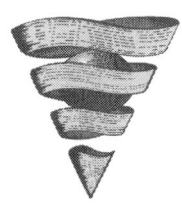

The first thing you have to know is yourself. A man who knows himself can step outside himself and watch his own reactions like an observer.
-Adam Smith

To the mind that is still, the whole universe surrenders.
-Lao Tzu

He who wishes to be obeyed must know how to command.
-Niccolò Machiavelli

Adam Smith

Delay not; swift the flight of fortune's greatest favours.
-Seneca the Younger

All of humanity's problems stem from man's inability to sit quietly in a room alone.
-Blaise Pascal

The more man meditates upon good thoughts, the better will be his world and the world at large.
-Confucius

The highest and most beautiful things in life are not
to be heard about, nor read about, nor seen but, if
one will, are to be lived.
-Soren Kierkegaard

It is the mark of an educated mind to be able to
entertain a thought without accepting it.
-Aristotle

The key is to keep company only with people who
uplift you, whose presence calls forth your best.
-Epictetus

God always strives together with those who strive.
-Aeschylus

He conquers who endures.
-Persius

The wise does at once what the fool does at last.
-Baltasar Gracian

Wise men speak because they have something to say;
Fools because they have to say something.
-Plato

The great use of life is to spend it for something that
will outlast it.
-William James

A good general not only sees the way to victory; he
also knows when victory is impossible.
-Polybius

Everywhere man blames nature and fate yet his fate
is mostly but the echo of his character and passion,
his mistakes and his weaknesses.
-Democritus

To become truly great, one has to stand with people,
not above them.
-Baron de Montesquieu

Diogenes

Wise kings generally have wise counselors; and he must be a wise man himself who is capable of distinguishing one.
-Diogenes

Patience is necessary, and one cannot reap
immediately where one has sown.
-Soren Kierkegaard

At his best, man is the noblest of all animals;
separated from law and justice he is the worst.
-Aristotle

To lead people, walk beside them. As for the best
leaders, the people do not notice their existence ...
When the best leader's work is done, the people say,
'We did it ourselves!
-Lao Tzu

The measure of a man is what he does with power.
-Plato

To do great things is difficult; but to command great
things is more difficult.
-Friedrich Nietzsche

There are many who know many things, yet are
lacking in wisdom.
-Democritus

All mankind... being all equal and independent, no one ought to harm another in his life, health, liberty or possessions.
-John Locke

Don't try to add more years to your life. Better add more life to your years.
-Blaise Pascal

The study of history is the best medicine for a sick mind; for in history you have a record of the infinite variety of human experience plainly set out for all to see; and in that record you can find yourself and your country both examples and warnings; fine things to take as models, base things rotten through and through, to avoid.
-Livy

What you leave behind is not what is engraved in stone monuments, but what is woven into the lives of others.
-Pericles

Whenever anyone has offended me, I try to raise my
soul so high that the offense cannot reach it.
-Rene Descartes

The mind is not a vessel to be filled but a fire to be
kindled.
-Plutarch

For a man to conquer himself is the first and noblest
of all victories.
-Plato

Talent hits a target no one else can hit; Genius hits a target no one else can see.
-Arthur Schopenhauer

Anyone can hold the helm when the sea is calm.
-Publilus Syrus

So we must work at our profession and not make anybody else's idleness an excuse for our own. There is no lack of readers and listeners; it is for us to produce something worth being written and heard.
-Pliny the Younger

Arthur Schopenhauer

The greatness of a life can only be estimated by the multitude of its actions. We should not count the years, it is our actions which constitute our life.
-Gottfried Leibniz

He who has learned how to obey will know how to command.
-Solon

The only thing permanent is change.
-Immanuel Kant

To lead people, walk behind them.
-Lao Tzu

Always desire to learn something useful.
-Sophocles

Excellence is an art won by training and habituation.
We do not act rightly because we have virtue or
excellence, but we rather have those because we have
acted rightly. We are what we repeatedly do.
Excellence, then, is not an act but a habit.
-Aristotle

Consider before acting, to avoid foolishness: It is the worthless man who speaks and acts thoughtlessly.
-Pythagoras

When Heaven is about to confer a great office on a man, it first exercises his mind with suffering, and his sinews and bones with toil; it exposes his body to hunger, and subjects him to extreme poverty ; it confounds his undertakings. By all these methods it stimulates his mind, hardens his nature, and supplies his incompetencies.
-Mencius

IX
May Your Intentions Be Noble:
Book of Visionaries

When we build…let it not be for present delights nor for present use alone. Let it be such work as our descendants will thank us for, and let us think…that a time is to come when these stones will be held sacred because our hands have touched them, and that men will say as they look upon the labor, and the wrought substance of them. See! This our fathers did for us!

-John Ruskin

Robert Kennedy

Each time a man stands up for an ideal, or acts to improve the lot of others, or strikes out against injustice, he sends forth a tiny ripple of hope, and crossing each other from a million different centers of energy and daring, those ripples build a current that can sweep down the mightiest walls of oppression and resistance.
-Robert Kennedy

I suppose leadership at one time meant muscles; but today it means getting along with people.
-Mahatma Gandhi

Carry out a random act of kindness, with no
expectation of reward, safe in the knowledge that
one day someone might do the same for you.
-Princess Diana

Forgiveness liberates the soul. It removes fear. That
is why it is such a powerful weapon.
-Nelson Mandela

Grant me courage to serve others; for in service there
is true life.
-Cesar Chavez

Martin Luther King Jr.

A man dies when he refuses to stand up for that which is right. A man dies when he refuses to stand up for justice. A man dies when he refuses to take a stand for that which is true.
-Martin Luther King, Jr.

Nothing in the Golden Rule says that others will treat us as we have treated them. It only says that we must treat others in a way that we would want to be treated.
-Rosa Parks

The man who promises everything is sure to fulfill nothing, and everyone who promises too much is in danger of using evil means in order to carry out his promises, and is already on the road to perdition.
-Carl Jung

It always seems impossible until it's done. *-Nelson Mandela*

Few will have the greatness to bend history itself; but each of us can work to change a small portion of events, and in the total; of all those acts will be written the history of this generation.
    -Robert Kennedy

About

MICHAEL J. ELLIOTT, a speaker and writer, is the creator of The Michael Elliott Podcast and founder of Pen & Mane and Idea Zero.

www.michaelelliott.net

www.penandmane.com

www.ideazero.co

Index

A

B

F

G

H

I

J

K

O

P

R

W

Y

Photo Credits

Chapter 1. Cornerstone: Book of Divinity

Image 1: "Joan of Arc" by John Everett Millais is licensed under CC BY 2.0
Image 2: "Sainte Thérèse" by François Gérard is licensed under CC BY 2.0
Image 3: "Sermon on the Mount" by Carl Bloch is licensed under CC BY 2.0

Chapter 2. Light in the Darkness: Book of Poets

Image 1: "Edwin Markham" by McMichael & Gro is licensed under CC BY 2.0
Image 2: Photo by Simon Fitall on Unsplash.com
Image 3: Photo by Tim Trad on Unsplash.com
Image 4: Photo by Willian West on Unsplash.com

Chapter 3. The Crown & Scepter: Book of Kings

Image 1: "Napoleon I in Coronation Robes" by Anne-Louis Girodet de Roussy-Trioson is licensed under CC BY 2.0
Image 2: "A colossal statue of Akhenaten from his Aten Temple at Karnak" by qwelk is licensed under CC BY 2.0
Image 3: "Portrait of Alfred the Great" by Samuel Woodforde is licensed under CC BY 2.0

Chapter 4. Pens, Paper & Destiny: Book of Authors

Image 1: "Portrait of Dostoevsky" by Vasily Perov is licensed under CC BY 2.0
Image 2: Photo by Freddie Martyn on Unsplash.com

Image 3: "The Plays of William Shakespeare" by John Gilbert is licensed under CC BY 2.0
Image 4: Photo by Pedro Nogueira on Unsplash.com
Image 5: Photo by Michal Grosicki on Unsplash.com
Image 6: Photo by Serkan Turk on Unsplash.com

Chapter 5. Folk Wisdom: Book of Proverbs

Image 1: Photo by Hollie Harmsworth on Unsplash.com
Image 2: Photo by Stephen Leonardi on Unsplash.com

Chapter 6. Charting the Course: Book of Patriots

Image 1: "General George Washington" at Trenton by John Trumbull is licensed under CC BY 2.0
Image 2: "President John F. Kennedy speaks at Rice University" from NASA is licensed under CC BY 2.0
Image 3: "Abraham Lincoln" by Alexander Gardner is licensed under CC BY 2.0
Image 4: "The Roaring Lion" by Yousuf Karsh is licensed under CC BY 2.0

Chapter 7. When Art Speaks: Book of Zeal

Image 1: "Road with Cypress and Star" by Vincent van Gogh is licensed under CC BY 2.0
Image 2: "Portrait of an Old Man in Red" by Rembrandt is licensed under CC BY 2.0
Image 3: "Wolfgang Amadeus Mozart" by Barbara Krafft is licensed under CC BY 2.0

Chapter 8. Philosopher's Stone: Book of Wisdom

Image 1: "Profile of Adam Smith" by Cadell and Davies is licensed under CC BY 2.0
Image 2:"Diogenes" by Jean-Léon Gérôme is licensed under CC BY 2.0
Image 3: Photo by Justin Kauffman on Unsplash.com

Image 4: "Portrait of Arthur Schopenhauer" by Ludwig Sigismund Ruhl is licensed under CC BY 2.0

Chapter 9. May Your Intentions Be Noble: Book of Visionaries

Image 1: "Robert F. Kennedy" by Warren Leffler is licensed under CC BY 2.0

Image 2: Rev. Martin Luther King, head-and-shoulders portrait, seated, facing front, hands extended upward, during a press conference / World Telegram & Sun by New York World-Telegram and the Sun staff photographer: DeMarsico, Dick, photographer CC BY 2.0